THE GLACIER'S DAUGHTERS

The Glacier's Daughters

David Brendan Hopes

The University of Massachusetts Press   1981

Library of Congress Cataloging in Publication Data
Hopes, David B.
The glacier's daughters.
I. Title.
PS3558.06343G59   811'.54   81–7612
ISBN 0–87023–339–4   AACR2
ISBN 0–87023–340–8 (pbk.)

FOR TOM

Contents

October

It's nuthatch on the box elder outside the window.
He's making his clown voice, *nnink, nning, nnink,*
pecking for grubs, seeds, scraps.
The first snow powdered down
last night while he slept, and as
birds have dreams there's snow in his song now.

Nighthawk heard it. He is gone.
Warbler heard it. She is gone.
Thrasher went. Finch went.
You could hear them at night, little bells
so far off you thought they were the stars ringing.
I sat on an èmpty hill and said goodbye.

The geese, like tragic actresses, keep nothing to themselves.
They beat down the center of the air
crying, and crying, how the white north
snaps behind them, how their nests are shoveled under,
how their circle is broken
by fox, bullet, and cold.

The geese, like the practiced keeners my great-grandmothers
used to pay when they had
no more salt to cry with,
bark for us all, uninhibited, bleating
on God's doorstep how He has wronged us,
how we suffer in His circles, round and round.

On Salina Street the hag with a hollow for a left eye
cries Jesus, Jesus, come and be saved.
She puts on her black coat.
Her old hand is nail and January to the bone.
Put a coin in her talon, a cold coin.
Take her pamphlet and let it ride the wind

as the geese ride, flapping, rattling.
Put a coin in the black mouth
and hear it cry Jesus Jesus,
hear it cry Jesus Jesus.

I swear the geese and the nighthawks and the hags
must cry something different when they come home

with the sun pulled up behind them
and the long hills waking from the five month bad dream.
I have not heard it in so long.
I hear the nuthatch in the box elder outside the window,
laughing, scrounging. He stays and dies,
or stays, and stays.

November

1

I recall now when it started,
this obsession with ice, this bringing
all thoughts back at last to the place
where everything is still and cold.

It was on the pond late afternoon,
a few minutes only before night.
The geese stayed there all winter
because of the corn fields sloppily harvested,
the gentleman farms used to lying fallow,
where the geese could waddle up, and eat.
It was not so far north then.
It was my pond. No one could shoot them unless
they threw themselves in the peril of the air.
Then it was cold one week, two weeks end to end.
The snow sang when I walked from house to shed.
My breath made gray sugar on the windows.
I heard it. I rubbed my hand on the rime
until it melted and I looked out.
I saw a goose on the pond fighting the dogs.
She was not moving, just her wings and neck,
the snake-neck flailing and stabbing,
her tongue arched like a catapult
against the bottom of her beak.
Now a goose in her fury drives off one dog,
two, more if she's brooding.
Four farm dogs were yapping on the ice.
I yelled "fly!" until my breath covered up the glass.
I ran out yelling "fly!" until I was on the pond.
The dogs would not give way, blooded.
I saw them, quiver-paw, snarling.
They let me close enough to see
her feet frozen solid in the ice.
I let them gnaw her down to ankle bone.

2

The flock settled when the dogs went home.
They were not at ease. The pond was a road
then any enemy could cross.
They gabbled all night, the lone gander
honking and squawking out toward the edge.
There are two things certain:
There is no silence among geese.
They kept me almost waking,
their necks craned, making the same sound
over to each other.
I picked out the gander's high drone
out of all of them, monotonous, obsessive,
scolding, even, if they turned too quiet.
I would go out at morning and sledge a hole,
sledge open water.
The other thing: they mate for life.

3

Long fall, Thanksgiving Day, the
zinnias in the gardens just barely dead.
Sun, breeze from the southwest
as though there were a sea there.
Each day like this is one for us.
I was out hiking early between two green lakes.
I heard a lone goose, a big Canada,
rolling on one good and one stiff leg,
too deep in the thickets to try his wings.
Shot, I guess. Blood stained his breast
where it met the leg, the feathers blown away.
I walked over to him. He walked to get away.
I ran; he ran, hissing.
I ran him to the lakeshore
where from under the branches
it was suddenly clear, and he
beat his wings on pebbles, on the water,
lifted heavily over the circle of hills,
shot off southward without another sound.

Whether he made it I don't know,
but he is free of here.

4
Sometimes I think I hate them.
The wind is angry, but it takes them home.
The snow is on us.
One step, two steps,
we have not moved.

Birdbones

The girdle is a grass leaf dried and curled.
Spine's whittled to a splinter, a thorn.
Clavicle is a taut hair holding without weight.
Wing blades are a folded feather, in a stiff wind
almost flying by themselves:
girder, crossbeam, strut, the bones of birds,
swallow bones, catbird bones, willing to bear nothing,
made to lift; with that furious heart behind them,
lighter than air, nimbler than light, made to
hover, veer, power, descend, home in, stoop, evade.
Against them there is no force: hammered, they leap;
tumbled, they gather and bunch back;
galed, they seize the whirlwind and rise.

Wind sledged the ash tree.
Its leaves went up and its wood went down,
a great wind, and the limbs were sailing.
In the space from which the ash had fallen
I saw swifts climb like black sparks
from a steel-gray stack.
They were safe where they had been,
under eaves, in chimneys, but the wind taunted
and they laid their bones against it for delight,
those strands, those parings. They spiraled up
the funnel of the wind, black, gray, blue,
climbed to the shine above it,
took their pastime in the storm.

What is small enough to get around,
light enough to rocket over,
quick enough to enter by the worst door?
Cardinal, whipped by fire that first day,
stepped into the fire;
wren, seeing her smallness among the beasts,
put on fury like a coat of knives;
bunting lost heaven, brought it down;
kingfisher saw how the world prepares and
comes to nothing, poised above the water,

hovered, blue on blue, neither diving nor departing;
chickadee snatched seeds beneath the beating axe,
ripped thistle from the bear's pelt,
it is my world, my world;
thrush stole the songs, that night might think
the world sings against it all together;
killdeer learned deceit, drew the hunters
from her generations;
swift felt the hammer, stepped aside.

Remember this: there are no fables.
If you didn't hear the wind speak you were not listening.
If the stars did not warn you, you were
safe at home with the doors locked tight.
If you sought your soul and didn't find
a small bird beating straight home forever
where there is no road, you were seeking something else.
And each day impossibly they lie down in air.
They take their bit of earth up
high enough to serve, insubstantial, indestructible,
come down because the sky stops, not their bones.

Gale from the West

The geese, who from the ground seem
almost hovering, are stopped between
where they want and where the wind will let them.
Like a runnel thwarted by uneven ground,
they hammer north, veering northwest when
the gale lets up an instant, beating,
holding their sky, held north again,
remembering in their windward eyes the lakes of Canada,
northwest, northwest, like the runnel, feeling
every contour for a gap to pour through, northwest,
lakeward, bugling as though heaven could be shouted down.

Following

Sore knees bear,
lungs kick to rhythm,
eyes unfold to photons
boiling in the field. Roadbound.

Dave Hagerman died running,
well under forty and fit as wild deer.
This is the spot almost, the crown of this hill.
Behind him I try running at his break-heart pace,
harder, till my legs are stone
and then not legs at all;
harder till blood would burst my neck
and the long grade's bucking like a stung horse,
and I think of leaping as he leapt
off this road
up easy
as the white smoke falls into the sky.

Runner in Storm

Not the Nike waffles on this ice:
    Adidas, flat-soled, to hold me down;
shorts and sweatpants, T-shirt, close-woven pullover,
then a jacket to break the wind,
this huge wind, this gray scythe
mowing from northwest, chopping the oily puddles,
hammering old snow to iron and rusting it away,
smashing the hilltop maples until I wish
    for them the power to lie down
        in radiant compromise.

The storm is against us. I hear
    the maples crack and slip as I run by.
They are losing. Wind is everywhere, flowing,
sucking away until the wood has no
antagonist to strain against. It holds
a minute, snaps out and bursts.
There is something here that is too strong.
I run bent at the waist, face turned
    from the drive of rain, going a little
        the way the wind wants me,

        pushed to a new road, taking it.
    Poor trees. The gale is hard on my body,
and how much harder were there sixty feet of me
braced and rooted and even the hill
curving down and leaving me alone.
I can go pull off my wet clothes and make coffee.
Whatever the storm has done to the mountains,
I shall go my way.
    Be it a hammer, I am no anvil.
        Be it sickle and flail, I am no field.

        I will not stand for it. Move. Run.
    Good feet, let's speed now, the dog wind snarling,
the bull wind horning us aside.
It could charge all evening
and we'd still have rum to run.
Poor trees. They stand in combat, mortal, musical.

They are too strong, too just and vertical.
I twist to the road again,
    leaping downed lumber,
        and above me suddenly is a little hawk

        fuzzed by the straight rain, sailing.
    He oars the crest of the hill, lifts, drops,
soars flat out, stoops to the crumpled trees.
Hard as wind beats him, he beats back,
holds like blown flame,
and then he stands, eye, hook, hackle,
tense in the wind on my head's crown,
still in that whirling like a rip in heaven,
    so fleet the fleet wind lets him stay,
        and I am Homo in an allegory.

        caught between magnitude and motion
        in the adversity of wind.
Hawk says nothing on earth is quick enough.
Hawk says whatever strikes the ground is root and fetter.
Poor feet, I say, lift, lift!
Hawk shot down the slant of snowy land and I lost him.
My limbs are sorry for their pride before the lopped trees.
In their good shoes, their wind-turning jacket
    they take me down the hill
        behind the wind-wed hawk.

        From the bottom the storm's sweet and high;
    it sings in the conifers, the supple-branched.
Twigs and trash go sailing.
The storm is half way out to sea again.
I wrap my arms around me.
I am not quick enough to keep off the cold.
But we are all here, fingers and toes, mine, running.
I could climb that wind and ride,
    almost, were there not too much of me.
        I am not quick enough. Cold. Poor trees.

But I am strong enough, I think,
 tree-strong, hawk-quick as wind fades.
I break ice with the blows of my feet,
  find a good pace, to pass through the storm,
   laughing, upright on the beaten road.

The Burning City

In the picture Goya left unpainted,
there is a dark walled city on a dark hill,
a pale road leading down onto the plain.
The city is on fire.
On the road, a cloaked figure
drives a cart.
The cart too is afire.
The mules grin in fear.
The cloaked man looks neither
at the cart nor at the city,
unable to believe
he could not save his meager cartload.

Let us say there were deeds of valor in the city,
that the defenders made forever an example
of lost, heroic honor,
and men died saving strange men's children.
Yet someone escaped.
To establish a narrative: rich once,
it seems, or a looter,
or a gate-warden deserting his post.
He loses before us everything he saved.
He carries fire into the plain.

Let us say the man at last must jump or die.
He watches the mules plunge madly
across the plain, the fire teasing their heels, turning
their coats into itself.
One does not think he would be free
to walk away.
One sees him turn back to the city,
involved, by now, from gutter to tower.
Even Goya would not make this up.

Jack Rhymer

Who am I? A tramp, I guess,
booting the road among the moons,
sleeping by the stars and wandering
the wildernesses of strange rooms.

Jack the fix-it-man and Jack the pimp,
Jack driver, Jack snow-man, Jack racketeer,
Jack of the dim street where
I answer to most any name I hear.

Jack scholar I am, Jack of the books.
I have forgotten what they say,
but how they say it sticks with me
that I might twist it around my way.

Jack Rhymer at last,
son of desperate fathers for sure,
making high talk to put them in
so some of their voices may endure.

I've walked out and I have seen
the raree show and fraud.
By empty doors and neon signs
I cry the travesties of God.

I turned my heart toward the town,
seeing how its children cry
solitary, unloveable, and afraid
with their backs against the floating sky.

I put myself in peril of the night
seeking a god to bear the blame.
I put myself in danger of the street
to see shame walking unashamed.

Jack of Eden I was called
till hunger broke the spell;
Jack Galahad my name before
the Christ-cup sat on the shelves of hell.

Jack mystery you call me now.
Unlike the hallows of the emerald age,
I prophesy unto the world
the dispensation of rage.

Jack of lovers, king of hearts,
crazy in the wounded town,
waiting for glad day to come
and lay our midnight down.

I set myself to war with God
till God confronts the hopeless street,
sing in cul-de-sacs and bars
hosannas for my own defeat.

Visions from the Dreadful City

1

How does it survive, I wonder,
with its delicate ankles, in the potholes and grillworks
and trash and stairwells of the city?
How has it learned, this unicorn, so smoothly?
It picks its hooves up,
prances, as though place made no difference.
It colors the walls with its whiteness,
silver in the alleys like a rush of water.
A woman leads the unicorn.
She is secret in the eyes.
She stares at the pavement, slow as a pivot
at the center of the dancing beast.
It nudges her beautiful dress.
It prods her sweetly with its horn.
It wants her to mount and ride.
The lady and the unicorn pass through the city.

2

One night I saw what should have been all along.
The street was full of voices,
men, women, hand locked in hand, talking
as God taught them, voice sprung from heart
as white water from a troubled river,
want from beneath as spray rocked up and rainbowed.

Satan, too, upon the street was speaking,
but not as we expected.
Mouse in a corner, gnawing dry rind,
hissing *she will leave you, he will turn his back.*
The Ghost, too, upon the street was speaking.
He said, *comes mighty wind; do not let go.*

3

If soul were a homesick lady,
desire would be a steed to take her
out from the midnight city.
If God is God,
devotion is get up and ride.

4
Oh, the girls are fine,
black hose the pimps buy them,
none of them ugly like you hear about,
bring you coffee if the waiters won't let a drunk in.
Best fuck of your life, too.
     The wino moved beside me at the fountain.
I met one here, pretty, twenty bucks,
but I didn't have it, and we did it anyway.
Face broken by a john once. Jeeze-god
I bawled when I saw her.
Don't know what since. Maybe too drunk.
For God's sake kid, give me something.
     His hand snaked for my wallet pocket.
     I let him have what the bulge was.
     It was a map.
     He took it, unfolded, studied,
     set out walking.

5
Climb this hill and look.
What do you see?
A city, beautiful and deadly.
It is great. Go home.
Think of the hills of your own country.
Go home. The city says it:
we are very great for very long.
Such luck does not come twice.

6
Maybe the city argues us to heaven.
     It says, *anyone afraid is too rich.*
     It says, *hate is mist on glass. Wipe it away.*
     It says, *kiss bearing down, hard.*

It says there is a truth not in the flowers.
It says there was always a City in the Garden,
     sad lost Jerusalem,
     Jerusalem that shall be.

It says there is no way out but through.

7

Lay your head by me and listen.
My skin like the skin of a drum
will beat to you.

I am not glad here.
Love keeps me, the small of your hair,
how your forearm fits my throat in sleep.

But it is too close.
Where are they, my old selves,
wood, leaf, water?

Love will keep me
if you'd keep me with it, if you can take
what my flesh says when I sleep.

8

The man I saw on the street last night
would not want the reasons, were there any,
for his emptiness. He would fly up
to that window where he watched,
window yellow and shadowed
where there must be somebody.
If someone leaned out, lovely,
drawing a white comb through her hair,
he could say *lovely, lovely,*
wanting without hope to have,
wanting which is not overture to action
or belonging, but a sort of prayer,
wanting such that he could turn
home easy in the deepening night.

9

Because of my love,
because there was no lover,
he came to lie beside me,
hair mingled in hair,
his eyelashes brushing my closed eyes,
tongue to tongue, breastbone to breastbone,
down belly, stem and root.

His hand on the back of my neck
pulled me into him, like a dark cloud
blown into a bright cloud, and then both one brightness.

10

Always last in spring, the nighthawks
bunch like bees around incandescent clusters
of billboard lights, agile, wary,
two moons on their wings,
buzzing as they fly, scooping and buzzing,
trying the corners to be sure.

Nighthawk: swift, hungry:
he nests in the heights;
he crowns what is prepared;
he baffles with crowing the quiet of the dark;
he cries to the jammed streets,
there is room.

11
42nd Street

Inexplicable the joy,
walking out at morning in the strange huge city,
discovering that the street runs east and west
and the sun at the end of it
bursting as though he kept a secret all night,
and his light belting its way, strong, red,
from the river to the river,
and how to ransack trash cans is epic at that hour,
how I, with two donuts bought with my own money,
turned homeward, not fearing any place again.

THE GLACIER'S DAUGHTERS

Hylas

Ten thousand years a mile high mount of ice
    sweat in spring a river from its face,
        the torrent gnawing pools beneath bare rock,
    melting back and gouging, two pools, three,
a ring of cold lakes built of loosened water.
    The streams, like cosmos in a Hindu parable,
        leapt out when night began to dance
    between bare heaven and bare cliff,
dead land brazen with the pang of thaw.

    Even then the peepers sang in March
        over drum-falls and the groaning ice,
    over the hammer that beat back each spring
from the advancing shadow of the trees.
    Peepers broke the rime to crawl up and call.
        They bore crosses on their backs, desire
    in the tiny bubbles of their throats.
They chirred the lost flocks home.
    They bloomed and furled their music like loud flowers.

    Long before the ice failed they sang
    day and night or silenced for a time
in sequence, like wind passing shadow
    down a field of wheat, when a pair of mallards
        preyed the passage between reeds, with their
    sharp eyes, their hunger carried from the south.
Hunger is the fulcrum of the world.
    The world is cloud and marble.
        They wake to end it.

Peepers sing to generations of their kind
how they trilled the ice away, and Hylas Lord
    He thought rain in imitation
        of sung-backward ice,
    He rivered to ease the northland of the flowing cold,
He mossed to shatter rock to set the world upon,
    He heavened so the geese came home,
        He crossed whatever bore the sorrow
    of the night and sang.

If you are large enough to eat animal at all
    you eat the cross-back frogs.
        If you are heron, bittern, duck, bass, snake, bullfrog,
    raccoon, crow, great sucking water-bug,
anything, you devour and hunger and devour again.
    You come because they were here to eat.
        You come to close their circle.
    Gobble; there is still the tumult in your ear,
the peepers in their myriad myriads.

    They sing as you suck them down.
        Remember, they have changed the world by singing.
    They chirr between your teeth, before your cunning,
before hot brains that brought to earth
    a want that is not of the belly,
        before the ice that froze you,
    before the intractable north,
before the sour east black and frost,
    sweet southwest shimmery with rain.

    They sing before you neither changed
    by the change they make, nor fearful,
cross-backed, small enough to balance on a grass.
    In dead March night they grip the heart.
        They say *most well most well Awake*.
    Eat till you are sick full.
They are still the throng,
    invisible paradise of voices
        trilling down what ground the world away.

Under the Drumlin

I will tell you what lies under this hill
    worked and hammered by the old ice.
First: roots, bleached hairs and thumbs,
grass roots woven to a floor the mice walk on,
    cocks of wild carrot, pushing down, begetting,
        the weathered apple with burnt child's arms
    for roots, tingling at the tips
like nerves stung over and over.
    Roots cross and kiss. There is no way.

        Under roots—rock: agate, sulphur, turquoise.
These are lizards and moths that died before the cold.
Quartz where the moon was frozen.
    Marble, veined, bone-white where monsters,
        Titans, ground sloths, rebel angels fell to die.
If you think this is a fancy, dig a deep trench
in fall and watch what forces up in April:
    flowers like claws of gryphons,
        lichen like eyes on blind rock,

    stems reaching and groping, gnawing the turf,
crest-shaped, nape-color, green and watchful.
    Under them: black water.
        Hill floats on water as sailboat rides the quiver of a lake.
    It does not, like surface pools, reflect.
It sheds a blackness from its heart.
    Its light draws roots down.
        Water stirs the jewels and bones.
It is blown to vapor by the sucking vortex of the grass.

Saints discovered in old times
    that a ladder leads down from God.
        It soars through Powers, Thrones, Dominions,
    sleeps in the sedge.
Earth drops the stairway down into herself,
    the inverse, the secret circumference,
        Holy the Burning braced by Holy the Black.
    The Hand open at the top to give
is open at the bottom to receive.

The gestures are forever complete and indistinguishable.
    Tiny joints of springtails creak
    like fireplace cats'.
Beasts on their cilia dance at morning.
    Rock moves its deep thighs in the water.
        Think of water that stood in rainbow while
    the wind shook rain on one side, diamond,
and the sun the heavens on the other, gold.
    This is the sea that sleeps here.

        From the breast, the silence
    it is forced only by more water pouring down,
longing to lie unmoved with the weight of the hill
    on its face like the breath of a lover.
        Dance if we rise and dance if we sink.
    It is how the world is made.
There are creatures stalking in the dark.
    Their names, like true names of stars, are hidden.
        They are the suns that called us in the common night.

The Swimmers

Even at night the ducks are at work,
quiet and duck-shaped on the lake,
like complications in enormous black silk.
Night is heavier than day.
The waves are round-shouldered
where they shove the shore.
In storybook weather, the purple-brown light,
the water and the ducks discuss
their storybook histories:

how there is right,
how there is natural,
how a bird might rest sometimes upon the water
and the water delight in its diadem of bird.
Then the ducks and the water laugh.
Fire is in a bolt of black silk.
One voice bubbles from the bottom of the lake
and hawks down from the iron stars
and it cries *lie lie lie!*

The facts are pain and horror.
Ask duck bones secret in the lake,
ice-crushed and starved to paper
when the north stomped down.
Ask ghost elm riddled with her worms.
Ask these cliffs down-blow of the everlasting hammer.
When did sweet Christ put his thorns
between the roses and the north wind?
Lake's eaten with stars.

Brown ducks ride in a field of coals.
There are moments when the story book seems true.
Carp descends among the water lilies,
gold hidden in shadow,
stir of blossom not of any wind.
A child fishes from a willow-knee
and is fire between dark water and dark leaves.
The moment is a steel jaw. What lets down its fear
is swallowed. What lets its hate rest

is ploughed under new snow
with the mice, trilling its blood to glass.
Christ, when did you make
your enemies a liar and come down
against all theories on the clockwork earth,
flail asphalt to dark flowers,
transform blizzard to a curtain of descending light?
Horror and pain have grown to us
like arms to push the world away.

Dawn. A boy flies a kite,
a silvery kite, like a hook.
It floats over the lake and therefore in the lake.
Kite and shadow, hook and hook.
I see God coming like a carp
among the shapeless lilies. He moves them without touching.
I see God rising in the lake, shivering
the waters that shoot through the earth.
He sniffs hook with his great snouts and moves on.

I see a swimmer on the lake.
It is cold there, but he seeks for God.
Ducks on the surface, paddling, pretending
to believe that they are droll and happy.
Perch, carp, shiner beneath, sucker, dace,
bluegill, sunfish, cat, large-mouth, small-mouth,
loon when there's trouble in the north.
God's jokes but not God. Perhaps in the tension
between water and air, the dime-thin borderland.

He looks. Nobody lives there.
It is a fence to keep the lake from leaping to the sky.
In his fury the swimmer swims out, out,
beating the underwater with his arms,
cutting the glaze away until he must be
dead center, the secret heart
that he will have or die. He descends.
He stands up with his shoulders showing.
Duck shit. Shore mud. He has missed the middle.

The ducks close him in a little circle.
They want to share with him the stories
they have made against the hour of their horror.
They see the swimmer eye-to-eye now. They understand.
If he swims out again they follow him.
If he trudges home they sit on the shore and watch.
They want to say there is no right ever, so be at peace.
They wish to celebrate that he too failed
conspicuously. That is the armor, the cloak.

It is too ridiculous for anything but our
smirk beaks and looney voices, they say,
how lake boiled out of glacier
when glacier seemed a tall flame in the sun,
how bird beats from a shell into a shell,
the white clown face hidden in the depths and in the heavens,
how the swimmers cut cold water thinking to find
what we wanted always, earth, wind, water,
once to walk proud upon our home.

The Invalid of Park Street

Like stitches in a gown, holding sleeve to bodice,
lace to hem, crossed, close and tight,
    these lovers walk forever knuckle to joint,
      palm to palm.
    God builds them half,
makes them find a friend to arch them,
    shore them, finish them.
      The first day they stroll by
    touching elbows when they dare.

The second day they twine from shoulder to fingertip,
    walking, stopping, shocking the street
      with their pose when they halt
    like carvings of lovers who know they'll die alone.
The third day and after
    it is just the hands,
      the whole rush circled there,
    the surety that ten hooked fingers are enough.
There is nothing that would not break them if it could.

    One thing can.
      You may have seen me
    through my window that looks north onto Park Street.
You may have seen one hand at rest
    atop the yellow blanket,
      its satin border tucked in carefully
    where my wrist hits fabric.
You may have seen the rock garden
    someone put in underneath my window.

    so the alyssum, the assertive live-forever
    might taunt until the snow avenges me.
You may have seen the bird feeder
    against the window I can reach
      by leaning on two canes. They said birds
    would take my mind from me
and they were right.
    Consider the sunflower hull
      out of which a chickadee ate.

It is small and dry, its striped pattern
torn where she held it in one claw,
    hammered with her head until
        the meat stood bare.
    Consider the care, the caution of its making,
compact, enduring, praiseworthy in all parts,
    lacking no quality that should mark
        a fire-colored tree-sized blossom
    bound in a dish for a winter bird.

It does not yield up too soon,
    does not hold niggardly, but is free, full.
        It does not change the treasure in the dark of the hull.
    What was food at the opening
is food at the consummation.
    Without it, chickadee snuffs out.
        When I hobble to the window, the brash bird
    kicks, scatters seeds, shells,
shrills for more and waits on the rail

    while more is brought. She swoops
        against the lace of my cuff in her anxiety
    to be there first. She holds her ground against me.
She tells me if I linger too long
    with my shadow on the fresh seed.
        Her impertinence, like a soul's before God,
    is blessed. She flutes her whole-tone
from the mound of empties, taking the richness
    that is her right, scolding the mere bearer away.

    Chickadee, hook-hand passers-by, and I—
    we are of one ambition and one lineage:
Want. Want not in proportion to any need,
    want unreasonable and overflowing,
        our days and nights overshadowed with desire,
    and as we eat the hunger's keener,
as we embrace, the distance worse,
    as we clutch our hands are too small
        and the wind steals it away.

You may have seen the firemen's "I"
on the front door, the "I" decal
   for invalid, that they might know
     what bones burnt here,
   wren bones that stopped bearing me,
sticks, stalks, tinder.
   If you missed the useless fingers on the blanket,
     that would tell you, the great red "I."
   Hurry. Let me burn.

You guess right that I watch as you
   pride past yoked and doubled, your bones
     like beeches laughing when the wind comes up.
   From the liver-spotted parchment ivory
of the hand in the window you guess right
   that I watched your mothers
     in their willow-time with smitten boy-hands
   at their waists, and watched at last
black hair unwoman their upper lips,

   watched dugs like scout cows wobble out
     before them, keeping the world at udder's length.
   Doves and lions become cows and crows.
It may surprise you to learn it makes me sad
   to lie here and see you beautiful
     at the brink of all your loss.
   Your men will raise their fists
against the sows that swallowed up their loves.
   You'll circle like weasels afraid to strike.

     Yet each April you are here hand in hand
   and stupid with love.
Look at me. Would you come in
   as readily as you tend my flowers
     to kiss this sick wreck in its dreams?
   I used to think of the moon and stars
when they stooped low and in the north.
   They are the same distance from us all. I think of warnings
     to paste on your window when the fire goes out.

The Dusk of Animals

One evening on Tilden's Hill as I ran
    too far, pounding the black road,
        tendon fraying bone, muscle fisting under flesh,
    feet pistoning like exiles on a plain of stone,
in the midst of the last uphill disgust
    I saw the crest come like the shell
        of a black, slow turtle, plodding
    its ruined orchards through the sky,
and I was atop, and there was peace.

    Though it was too light yet for any stars
        I knew where they would come,
    white flocks, blue hornets, Venus over Tilden's shed
like moth wed in ecstasy to flame.
    Moth, birds, my turtle: I was over
        Tilden's Hill into the dusk of animals.
    Cows rode like clouds on the heaven of their little field.
The farm dogs lifted up their heads
    to see themselves when the stars came out.

    I heard thrushes in the thickets.
    They considered the hagiography of summer,
humbly, knowing that sparrow suffered all
    that they might loll upon the thorns and sing.
        The thrushes note the delusions of the cloudy cows,
    how the farm dogs have no ear
but are courageous before the adversary
    and do not, like them, go hymning south
        to feast amid the blossoms always.

    If the thrushes heard my feet they
did not put them in their song.
    I will put them in mine.
        Where the cows would sleep was purple.
    The space between my shoes and road was purple.
One dog rose from his purple
    to run beside me, and two of us
        were animal by animal until the stars
    came out to show us who we are.

Four-feet pawed along a little, and he said
    "I have seen a ghost once, white
        in its face, fire where animals have flesh,
    all edges and no sides."
I said, "It is the Holy Ghost, or it is winter."
    He said, "It went down the white hill
        crying when the birds froze, when the sky froze.
    I slept easy with the ice in my paws."
"It is the Holy Ghost," I said. "You are blessed."

    Four-feet kept beside and said,
        "I know the history of the grass,
    who died and how. I listen
in the dusk of animals into the bone.
    You are here to tell me of the ghosts.
        Two-feet, winter and summer
    come by here and comfort me.
I am a little brown dog
    with the hard earth dancing in my nose.

        So I told it. One ghost came from the glacier,
    Four-feet, one came from the Fire.
I will teach you.
    Fear stone, thorn, the cow's hoof.
        Fear your sad master when the winter's in him.
    But the Ghost is a field where
dead hair breaks to flame.
    He says "Get up and dance"
        and the dry bones dance.

    He calls "Four-feet, Four-feet,"
and you are His angel.
    He says "Two-feet," and I come to run
        beside you, animal by animal
    as though no hard Eden split us,
telling tales good animals tell at dusk
    in star-just-peeping purple upon Tilden's Hill,
        when Venus comes to comfort in her star,
    and thrushes think it has been this way forever.

Job from His Mountain

There are mountains in paradise.
   The highest go to the merry,
  for they saw true heaven from the first.
The next go to the sad-in-time
  and merry-in-the-blood, for they sat
    in the ashes and let it pass.
They that dwell on the mountains see
the light rise and the light lie down.
  The light does not fade, but turns its dance.

   And Job from his mountain sees
  how the foundations were laid sly and dark,
the battlements of ice above them.
  He knows the measure, the spring, the fastening.
   How the water sings behind its doors!
O, how in his seasons Mazzaroth climbs
the ranges shining, and the child crows
  cry in the widerness and are filled,
    each one of them.

  Job from his mountain blesses the sweet hills.
They are proof by their presence.
  They shall answer in the Consummation
   and only the sea's voice will speak after them.
  They bore the ice and for their anger
bear the flowers. We are not speaking
  of likelihood now, but of the hills.
   The work of the hills is watch, wait.
   The why of the hills is where they lead.

Job from his mountain blesses the trees
  who clap their hands in the heights.
   They climb the hills by resting on them.
  They receive their ornament of birds by waiting.
When the ice left they walked back
  generation by generation till it was earth again.
   They wed water and wind and make themselves.
  They ascend upon their own deaths, dead wood
upon dead wood into the stars of morning.

Job from his mountain blesses the wind
    and the limbs and waters and
sticks and stalks in the wind.
Wind is music when it strikes.
    All things have root to resist it,
        wings to ride it. Birds cling with claw,
    ascend with feather; tree roots and leaves;
Earth has her heart to anchor her,
    her hills to lift her up.

    Job from his mountain blesses the birds,
    and for the earth hills three birds most:
cardinal and thrush, the balancers,
    for the morning red and evening dapple,
        the forseers, singing at the gateways of the True Sun.
    Then hawk, who pulls the middle,
who draws the blue hills higher,
    who is their longing broken from its stone,
        the road they were rising to forever.

    Job from his mountain blesses False Solomon's Seal.
It is a two-thirds arch,
    a parabola broken by a spray of berries.
        Its curve is not completed in a space
    of dirt floor, but in
promissory seeds, in generations.
    Job from his mountain blesses
        our old selves who follow through the dust,
    who come to withered hills for bread of stone

and honey of the hawk's slant fading home
    by early night. Where there is nothing
        sow-thistle in a limestone cup is Covenant.
    There is always something green against the season.
Job merry on the unlooked-for hills,
    bless who bore me, grass, beast, woman.
        Hold me in them for a little while
    as the old earth holds her brood
till they are her again, green, forgetting.

Labrador Pond

In Labrador Pond the heron makes letters:
S for the stalking; *lambda* for the reaching out,
one foot where it was and one where it wills;
    lamed for the waiting, a wood heron
        not even wind ruffles, the water eyes
    behind the steel dagger of the beak,
holy, Hebrew, abiding the instant of the kill.
    It strikes. It is *alpha, aleph,* first.
        Psi airborne, the monogram of soul.

He is alphabet. He leaves to other things the words,
"hill," "heaven," "heron," even.
    Their weight is balanced in the mind where
        heron has no space between desire and fear.
    His singlemindedness is a variety of perfection.
He stabs and statues. He looks down
    or to the side and heaven is as queer to him as us.
        He casts his shadow on the lake.
    A shore-sound tingles the half of him that fears.

He splits two hills as he flies: Jones, Labrador,
    divides the ice-flattened valley,
        the ice-begotten oval in the center,
    the kettle lake that kept the cold
the Apriled glacier left behind.
    Seven hundred feet above the water
        the rag-tag forest of Jones Hill covers its scars slowly.
    From it everything is blue, a blue immensity,
except where wild mustard

    signs the fields in a golden tongue, changing irony
        to praise as the sun goes in and the sun comes out.
    Heron lifts from his everyday into the height,
his water skill turned to suit the wind.
    We will not forget he has been driven.
        We will not forget that before splendor was fear.
    The great bird dark in the glittering blue
would fold into the hill, invisible,
    would stalk in a cave of misty water.

But driven, still he is lord now in the
spaces of the wind.
What looks, looks after him
and will go home filled.
He sees flowers in the wood not yet drawn tight
from futile ploughlands: hawkweed,
wild rose, rose mallow, hop clover, vervain,
cup-flower, the score of thistles, moosewood, hazel,
the children of the great trees, climbing,

folding their fingers as one does when the battle
is fierce but plainly won.
He breaks above them into limitless air over Hogsback,
Morgan, the blue hammered hills,
their gouged-out ponds between their knees.
Heron bears the cipher of soul into the center,
over three counties, over Fabius, Pompey,
white towns nestled in the folds like toys
the glacier lost when it was called home.

At the pinnacle he turns back.
Heron declines from heaven, his brown wings *tau,*
the cross upon the column,
the descending firmament.
He glides to his image on the pond's face,
heron spread over heron, the wingbeats
indistinguishable though one is creator and one creation,
one the lover and one the caress of his love
upon the black face of the beloved.

As a star burns complicated fire without equations,
heron has no word but has the heart,
a blue heart equal to the wind, but home here.
He adores but is not fool.
He does not think ever that the cold lake yields,
It gives, or there is nothing.
It is frog-teeming, fish-full, prodigal,
unpredictable, and he returns bearing its
languages and allegories like stars on his blue back.

When he sleeps his wings are hunched like two hills,
　　curled at the base: *omega*.
Even in sleep the snake eyes scan the lake
　　for signs, watch the hills
　　　　look in like guests at a stranger's table.
　　Moon is a pond in the valley of the sky.
Clouds are her hills, struck silver
　　and flowered with the sprays of galaxies,
　　　　cool, perfect, and what bird lifts his wings there

　　nests in the night, that secret tree.
Heron is obsessed.
　　He has heard a hundred hills call him
　　　　for their ornament, brag to him of lakes
　　that breed and exude, of bogs
where he might glory in the clacking of his chicks
　　amid the trees. Yet he abides.
　　　　Labrador Pond gives as it pleases,
　　and withholds. It pleases.

In all ages it has not learned
　　how to scorn such love.
　　　　It loves back. It turns its face to heron
　　when he flies, lake heron under heron,
love so great that when the fisher-bird abandons it,
　　it takes whatever lover's left,
　　　　loves ice and turns to it,
　　is cold and death as it was heaven
and heron when the world was right.

Star-face

There is no republic of the soul.
There are the lords that take;
    there are the commons that accept.
      There are those that rage
    and those that count the hours.
Well lifts up better as
    a tower rises on a wall,
      as hawk on a wedge of cliff wind,
      as scent winds to night like tight silk.

Mind is forever trudging up and down
    with Jacob's angels on the stairs.
      It keeps its sense of the ascendancy of things.
    It knows the greater and the lesser light.
Shrub is a tent and tree a roof.
    Breeze on a pool is troubled silver,
      but storm unlocks the sea
    and its serpents clap their claws
to God as He grieves them.

    Mind's eyes are forever centered
      on Gold-face and Silver-face, sun, moon:
    he who drives the ice back,
she who beautifies it;
    he the jug of fire and she
      the basin that receives and cools to drink.
    They are right hand and left hand on the drum,
one to beat and one to soften,
    one to enflame and one to dream.

    Behind them is the one whom heart wants.
    Star-face. He is more black than fire,
more wandering than place to be.
    Star-face hung on heaven.
      Heart chooses him, for his fire is fleck and precious,
    for he is so far off he must descend
in a convulsion of fire,
    for fire is substance smelted to desire
      and purifies even in hell.

For he is a little star spaced from a little star
by nothing, and the cold of that hollow
    is the same cold heart sprang from
        in freezing time before the flowers.
For he is like the flowers of the earth:
five-point, six-point, white blades
    bristled from the core against the cold.
        He is like the sparrows that take wing by night
        and are not afraid because they are many.

If you thought a law is as good as an angel
    or proof as good as a star,
        consider how the birds go home in darkness
    in the cusp of winter, northward,
Gold-face, Silver-face ambushing them,
    and only Star-face able, his fire for milestone,
        his points ordering the mazes of the land,
    beating under the birds' caps what
the love-way is, the one road back.

    How can the sun love us?
        He gives because he is full to flowing.
    He is beauty without tenderness, bounty without need.
Consider how Star-face is light outposted
    in a wilderness of dark.
        He is hope chrysalised by cold, vacancy stopped
    at the moment of its triumph by a battlement of fire.
Where was Gold-face when ice ground down the grass?
    Moon preened her paring in the glass.

    It was Star-face in his sorrow who endured.
    He heard the seeds clenched in the ice.
He vowed they would be as he is,
    fire at core, five blades, six blades
        nimbused out against the adversaries.
    He swore the exiled birds should hear him
calling downward from the beatened land the way,
    that they should configure in the wind,
        themselves like stars, a zodiac of birds.

Before the spirit took on clay or ash tree
struggled skyward on its rungs of dead wood,
 Star-face split his light to close night in.
 He foresaw the heart, and made himself
as it would be, black pierced by burning,
beast at play upon the chasm.
 He spread himself for passage.
 He wrenched the tales until we took the void
face-on, and saw no night but heaven.

The Glacier's Daughters

Mother plasma. Father fire.
   He thundered and she sucked him down.
     See yourself in blue light on the water,
  the live heat, the heirloom of a trillion generations.
We are the bolt-born, lightened from the sleep.
   We are the horrible stirring, the wriggle out,
     Out, rising on the corpses of the first hour.
   The sea was eaten and the land was eaten
and it is not enough.

   We are an imperial family.
     Hill, cleft, we have them,
  sun, shade, sea-deep. Divide us,
we flow back. Burn us, we blacken
   and take root. Drown us, we fin, we gill.
     Starve us and we gnaw. Tiny teeth.
  Slivers of nails, burrowing back-paws.
We have cousins who uphold the roof.
   We have cousins who gambol in fire.

    First mother, Terra, the crone
  takes us for ornament gladly, that her face
alone is memorable among the drone stars.
   We are the flight which is repose between two dances.
    We are the weavers. Our eyes are on our legs.
   We bore with our tap root. We whiten the sea
when we breach above her to the moon's face.
   We hugged the pointless hills to ourselves,
    lance-leaved, multi-petaled, made them.

Under our black eye-spotted whirring backs,
under the hooves that buoy us over cousin grass,
  we have changed everything.
    It was deep and we dug.
  It was lofty and we lifted.
It was many and we multiplied.
   It was lovely and we took shapes to us
    that are the single loveliness forever.
It was winter and we died.

It was cold in the world and we waited.
　　The glacier was the night.
　　　It bore its ghosts and stars.
　　It was the strange time when our mother
turned her head and slept, and wept
　　in her sleep tears that hardened
　　　in the moon and crushed us.
　　We would not leave her. We dreamed
what we might be when the bad time left us.

　　Cliffbrake, birch, red cedar, saxifrage,
　　　wolf's claw, moonwort, bleeding heart,
　　bloodroot, bloodroot.
We are the glacier's daughters.
　　We rip the rock.
　　　We grow fingers where our hearts would be.
　　We work down, gripping, grinding stone to soil,
squeezing green from dark where nothing
　　moved since mountain danced up from the sea.

　　　Two fists hammer her, the sleeping mother.
　　Father is night and fury. We are the second.
We are fire in green gloves, wind in a cup of flowers,
　　bulging what the snow beat flat.
　　　Green, the glacier's daughters, giving back,
　　atoning for our father, for the sins of God.
Rock wears us in its nakedness.
　　Its shame is turned to forests.
　　　Its wounds run green and frill.

　　Climb this battleground, this withered rock,
among your sisters who have labored longer:
　　toothwort, ironwood, hart's tongue, bracken.
　　　We are first-born at the task, recovering,
　　amending all with sinew where our hearts were.
We fight for the garden lost by God's turned back,
　　against sleet, snow, the intolerable solstice,
　　　ever the ice-hill looming with its bastinade of stars.
　　We have made ourselves from nothing.

We cling to the cliffs and pity them,
    pity the brief oaks their beauty, how they
        out-grip God and how the least wears them away.
    We sigh to the hurt hills, "Pilgrim. . . ."
We are the foundation. Trees taste and stay,
    lavish trees heavy from south with their clouds of flowers,
        their arms rising to the sun as if they planned
    to climb forever, the roots
forgetting as they pour toward heaven.

    We come first in spring before they shade us.
        We are green through winter, remembering
    cold beside which this cold is a needle
in a sea of ice. We are the glacier's daughters.
    Grandfather fire is in us. Grandmother, the abiding.
        We reach out and take. We have
    turned winter into world again.
We fetch this hill from nothing.
    God howls and we suck him down.

When Sally Plays the Spoons

When Sally plays the spoons
Louis jingles good silver money
in his pockets, his deep old pockets,
and he says *Honey, Honey.*

When Sally plays the spoons
her bones go *ratatata rata-tat,*
and the men at the bar look round
and say "What do you think of that?"

When Sally plays the spoons
Old Dave likes everything he hears,
picks a few more pockets
and he buys a round of beers.

O when Sally plays the spoons
the room goes *ratatata rata-tat*
and the floor boards ask the feet
"Now what do you think of that?"

And she goes *drum drum,*
she goes haily rain,
she takes the ratatat apart
and bangs it back again.

And the Old Man he says
I'll think up tunes and tunes,
O Sally, but you gotta
play them, play them spoons.

Lament for Turlough O'Carolan

Late it was in the night, with the wind
beating in a circle like a shot bird
and the bittern flapping from the reeds and
hammered down and in the flat black storm I heard
a harper harping for the dead
and I staring straight up in my bed.

You promised us next years like a farm
set about with orchards and a trim house
on it carved to the eaves with gryphons and
fine ladies, with twenty windows facing south.
And now in ghouly night, Turlough,
you put your bones to your lips and blow.

You promised a green tree and shade for
our journeys. You promised that it would be
seed time and summer and harvest unless
God Himself turned English. You must harp for me.
I want the paradise you sold
for a pocketful of peddlar's gold.

It's early in black morning I hear
the harp coming in like the wind off waves.
Where is your minstrelsy, Turlough? I walk
the same walk, stitch the old stitch. O be brave
my heart: the wind's not come quiet
though the harper's gone who lied through it.

"Si Bheag, Si Mhor"

Can't you hear the whistles and pipes
braying in the broken green?
My love, lay off birth and death
and dance for all the time between.

Bring us a jug for warming up
and a lie to light the night.
Love and Carolan are tart blind boys
and make us dance by bitter light.

Bring us a flag to mend our clothes
and a crown to beat the time on.
Push out a tale to fill the gaps
the gentle hearts are gone from.

I've put on my lightest shoes
and the hard stars all climb home.
I'll dance with God and all His saints
and I will dance alone.

"Planxty Irwin"

Sometimes the music's in the room
and you're alone and there's nothing
but to let it down and dance.
And I tell you it's fierce to dance
when your father's on your back
and your mother's on your back
and seven hundred years when
your people were alive with nothing to tell
but beaten princes and the bare hills.

They say the best tune's scratched
from the fiddles of blind men,
for the blind can see the worst coming
hump and bump over the dark fields.
Who plays must dance,
and the blind can jig off—cliff and sea—
too far ever to come back, just music in their ears.
I want to go that way, I said.
So did they all.

Testaments

Those sour harpers, their mouths metallic
from the taste of God, their cassocks bloody
from who knows what deed commanded and accomplished
in the dead of night, fuming like brimstone bellows,
they were not given to understatement.
But they did not see me. "Great Fish" was sufficient
for their purpose, supposing Jonah's journey
was an allegory for the flight, and restoration,
of the soul. Not even Jonah saw me coming
when I shadowed that toy ship as the whirlwind a lost sparrow.
He would have forgotten his shame, forgotten Nineveh
and Yahweh the Testy and sunk back to his babyhood for
drawn-out vowels of wonder at my firmament of shining scale.

I am a great fish as heaven is a great roof,
as Ocean is a great green drink.
But the Lord God He stirred me,
and the Lord God prodded me as a boy
some fat pond carp and said, *I have a morsel for you*.
I ate, and had three days a roaring in my belly
as though I'd swallowed a harrow or a star.
My belly growled *deliver me!*
and I belched *Nineveh! Nineveh!* into the deep.
God tickled me into the shallows
and delivered me at last.
Jonah staggered in the searing light, snow-white,
half digested, splashing shoreward without looking back,
to prophesy to a dry, doomed city, to come to think,
after the talent of his kind,
that I was a dream, a great fish story.

Where is Nineveh that great city?
They heard, put on their sackcloth, and were
ground to cinders just the same.
My gut is wiser than the prophets.
It has heard footsteps in its secret places,
heard someone cry between its bones.

It is not taken in by the mercy of God.
I shall rise from the fathoms at the end
and you shall remember everything.

2

Do you think you hate me?
You are a whelp in hate, a soft white egg.
I have fattened on it for a million years,
am old and terrible in hate.
I suck my tail and go round the stars.
Hatred began when I saw him slide among the orchids
in my colors, down the curves of that new tree,
hissing *Eve, Eve,* my fine coils stolen
to adorn his vermin heart,
and the beasts of the garden drawing back
as though I had given him merrily
this form to do his helling in.
Behind my Aztec eyes I hate forever.
You have nothing like it. Hide in your houses
and make tales from it to scare the children.

I vanish in the weeds when she walks by.
She bellows, and you come with sticks.
I do not blame you.
Look close. Of all creatures of that garden
was there one more beautiful? Am I not
the chessboard of the Lord, the rainbow of all weathers,
the palette fresh and looping among flowers?
No one sees me but draws back weeping and remembers.

The Serpent. The Great Dragon.
I shall take these names back from him.
On the Last Day I'll coil cunning in the grass,
strike when he comes hissing in his pride,
in my colors, in the glory of my name.

3

I had come to bathe my feet in the shallows.
Two men in the water, many on shore.
I descended as I do light as a petal,
my wings held up a little, my sweet voice.

From the murmur I knew I had
stumbled in the heart of something.
Voices rolled down Jordan like a rain.

Holy Ghost, I said, Holy Ghost,
what have I done?

It was well done, He said, *most well done.*
And I flew off.

FIVE NEO-PLATONIC COMMENTARIES

1 Helioselenus

The stone called Helioselenus, i.e. of the sun and moon, imitates after a manner the congress of those luminaries, which it images by its color—Proclus

Waking. The first thing, I am aware of cold,
everywhere, and one greater cold creeping in from outside.
My body curls in the sleeping bag
like a log on a dying campfire,
the outside freezing and the inside hot,
fire feeding on the proximity of fire,
red faults radiating out to warm the knobs and planes.
The greater cold is where my hand reached out at night.
It lay in the moonlight, lies there now
too numb to be moved, the rotting moon
rocking on the west and the fresh sun
warping the horizon still lower east.
The hand: for a moment it is ice white, flame red.
The sun at the finger tips works down.
The moon swims in the gulf of the palm.
Then everywhere is fire. I pull it in.
It lies against my body, cold, like a
diamond or a demon child.

2　The Cave

We entered from the north.
There were two sounds: water, bees.
There was one engorging dark.
The water came both from outside
and from farther down,
splashing, flowing. The bees
moled in from the field above,
laid down their honey in live rock
where cold and enemies never come.
We had not seen them in the field,
not seen them dropping, laden,
where there grew no flower.
We heard them droning on the roof,
the sound, if we did not keep our
thoughts on edge, like the cave
speaking one syllable, invariable, continuous.
It was purple beyond the reach of our lamps.
We aimed the flashlights out, pretending
to look for blocks or ways,
but looking at the purple,
purple like the robe of someone leading us
just out of sight.
At what seemed the bottom was a clear pool
shallow over pebbles. I dipped my hand in.
Under the water I was the color of the stones,
pale, clean. At that moment
I was frightened, and at home.

3   Webs

By morning the webs were woven again:
silver, gray-silver, silver-white,
one nearly red, whether by species
or the angle of the light.

Like creatures spawned purely by the dawn,
the webs and threads festoon
an empire in the corners of the air
that will be invisible at noon.

Straight light misses the complexities.
But by this bend in the sun
it is plain by whom the forms
are imagined and begun.

By this twist I remember that they weave
and forget they weave to kill.
The achievements puts on flame.
The agents are decorous, invisible.

4   The Dry Lake

Limestone it might have been, or gravel.
But it is finished now.
Each year they quarried closer to the lake,
so at last it was a green deep bowl, one half
rim sheer cut, the other half a level of trees
stretching out toward Windham and the Quarry Road.
The damp black cliff face should have told them.
The leakage should have said *too close*.
On the day it would take no more, the rim gave
and the water fell four days and nights.
Boys rode from town to watch it,
green by day, black tilted tabletop by night,
lustrous, hissing so long the people started
from their beds when at last they did not hear it.
Farms of two counties failed
in the slurry of the broken lake.
Before it was safe, the boys crept in
to harvest fishbones from the mud, to gather
shells of turtles from whom the whole world
gushed away and the terrible light came over.
Fall, spring, as long as there were any to remember,
ducks circled, saw the silver gone, flew on.
The wandering moon came looking for herself
where water was.

Odd how long it took the bottom of the lake to flower.
Mullein tried. Summer withered her.
Charms of finches dropped, found nothing,
bunched on the thistles of the rim again.
Stones that held deep water
lifted their dry mouths to the rain.
Sun bent over, but the plain did not
shoot his light back, kept it, drinking, drinking,
until the fire was in the ground.

One morning there I saw three birds.
Eye streak, blue bullet body, puddleside blaze-throat,
rump white yellow in full sun: myrtle warbler.

Behind the bird I knew there came
a dark bird and a gold bird beside.
These birds were not in any book.

In autumn the tracks are frozen for a while
until the sun comes out. I went early.
Hunters were already there, their
red and yellow shell casings caught in white grass.
That first freeze was so thin the raccoon broke it
walking puddle to puddle toward me,
dragging something, it seemed,
or with a shadow like a black veil clamped behind him.
He came too close, and I moved to let him know.
He'd known the whole time. He turned.
His backside and hind leg were sheared away
by bullets, his organs caught in the air
like eyes in a sudden lift of headlights.
The guns began again, far off by the road.

I dreamed of the lake, how I would
bring the waters back, how I would
dive in to make it right, and the moon
would walk upon her mirror, and the sun
would find himself somewhere between the seas.
If a man shouts from the south of the dry lake
the words do not come north,
unless the space has something of its own to say.
That night was a great roaring.
Wind spun in the frozen bowl.
I went hollow and the wind blew through.
I went to the rim and leaned till
only roaring held me up.
Snow came to the great drum, hushing.
Full, it was full past the rim into the blank sky.
I turned from it and went home all night.

5 Stars

i

This is the high hill of Thornden Park.
The lights of the city skirt it, wheel it,
as though it were a dancer's body,
as though it were the axle-tree.
Above the slowly turning city sit
two bands of black, the lower one to mark
how far our radiance extends;
upper, like a seam in a flawed black garment,
marks where heaven ends.
Above the seam, the firmament.

Low down, the flights of darkness stop.
Light streaks hawking to the top.

Sometimes we did not work backward,
divining best from what we guess of least,
but saw their floating home, the burning city,
the great house lamped and glassed, the country
of Dominion and Principality and Beast
held swinging there by Love and set to dance by Word.
Some star, some adamant Intelligence
looks down to watch the light
below his shining town, across the black fence.
He sees it is there as it is amid the night,

the people of that place walking, looking out, awake,
blazing the dark with the fire they make.

ii

The first star was snow-on-the-mountain.
He grew green, white, holy.
He led the old ones home.

The second star was ragged-robin.
She grew green, red, holy.
She led the children home.

The third star was elecampane.
He grew green and gold and holy.
He led the young men home.

The fourth star was gentian.
She grew green and blue and holy.
She led the women home.

Fifth star was amaranth.
He grew green and green and holy.
He is a fountain made of stars.
He led my love, led home,
the long, good way.

Hawkweed is a swift star, and he hunts.
Bramble is a winding stair. She finds.

iii

I am tired of the things of earth.
It is a film between two firmaments.
Tell me what is under the earth.
Gold that is dim rock,
diamond that is dust,
rain that lost its way,
root that sleeps,
bones that lie dim and dust and lost, and sleep.

But it is such a little space,
there, the underneath.
Tell me where they go when it is filled.
Gold is the sun and leaps up.
Diamond cuts dark; it vaults; it flames.
Water rills home to her kindred,
deep into the deep that was.
They light; they sheathe; they fountain.

Root—remember root?—she bore
a small star on the tip
and called star flower, and she drew
the flower into her and slept.
Flower shone deep a while. Bones saw,
and flowers taught bones the way home,

where they were mounting on their tired toes,
where they were watching and it still was dark,
where they rose at last, stars at their eyes
and fingers always.

Winter Birds

1

Don't think the stars and moon are all
that set out sailing over Thornden Hill
this last August night.
I have never said what is in my heart.
I have pointed to the birds
and let them have the summarizing words
as their wintery lives are blown apart.
Now listen. That is the compassing call
of nighthawk filling his belly for the long flight.
He is doing what we all soon will.
He finds the way by voices. They touch
roof and wall. By his cries
he knows how distant and how much.
He fills up heaven till the echo dies.

2

Do you think because you suffered for love
nothing more will be asked of you?
Do you think because your beauty was besieged
an hour, an afternoon, a week or two,
that all the high dead lovers are appeased?
Because your bones ride stark in your cheeks for love
do you think one cord of the net is eased?
I say there are nine hells for every one
you bawled away behind you.
You think you have endured. You have not begun.
If you saw where the road was you went not in love.
If it is gentle, it is through.
Do you suppose that what you gave, and lost, and missed
will keep you from knotting the blankets in your fist?

3

A lover taken in winter is an ice-bound harbor,
a she-wolf, a bolted door.
A lover taken in winter is a lock
and a well-stocked house
and a guarded door.

64

she will not give. She will not lose.
A lover taken in winter is amaranth.
She is a high wall and a black door.
A lover taken in winter
is a ruby, a shelter, a knife,
a golden door.
Love begun in winter is a fox
and a prophet and a blind door.
He closes. He survives.

4

In Baltimore the mockingbirds
told in every language but words
of bird, and air, and bird in air,
and how the flocks go when there's nothing left.
One at my window sang *Wake, awake,*
see the colors that the mornings make
to sharpen the delight of my inveigling black-and-white.
Look quick, while all my magic's left.
Any bird that labors in any tree
you'll hear better boiling out of me.
My mimicry is best. Leave aside the rest
that have only genuineness to recommend
them when all the songs are at an end.
Come out on your heavy feet and drink the melodious deceit.

5

Pure as the note of a bird, sometimes,
the sound of bark scraped on bark,
wood bowing wood.
There are strings in oaks, reeds in pines,
percussion in the cedar dark
below the cliffs, where trees that withstood
are struck by trees that were defeated
by winter and relaxing rock.
All work to bring silence from their noise.
Shaft smooths trunk; the brush repeated
planes the gnarl; the wind-blown shock
flattens, dies. Uneasy with their own voice,

the solitary outlast all the rest.
They've seen the weasel led by singing to the nest.

6

There is something rhetorical, of course,
in repenting love for its perversity
after it has been loved out,
after drawing the tingle of tongue and snout
as far as the night will let them go.
I did not know what roads could be
except the one that wound to me;
I did not see how time rolls us about
until all the rose sweet lovers go
bud to briar and bloom to stump, their course.
It is not yet so late that I'll extol
the suitable over what hurt best,
nor forget how flesh followed soul
sucking the salt sweat from the breast.

Something of the Flowers

I have earned something of the flowers,
not picking,
not bruising,
stepping carefully,
inviting them to stand in for spirit
and excellent women, for virtues, years,
the temporary stars.
I've learned their names,
learned them better when the books were wrong,
leaned close, and listened.
I've wandered to their beds by night
noiselessly as long birds hunting with their
eyes afire in the dimness,
stepped lightly between wet stems, careful
as the earth was live black lace,
the sky a shakable black bloom.
I bent over shut eyes of the flowers.
I breathed them in.
I decided they must be wanderers and pilgrims,
seeking in the dirt, and sleeping;
seeking in the wind, and blown away.
I thought they must be women
changed to flowers to bless them.
(How lord the night enfolds her,
hand on her, breath in her, dark to her dark.)
I thought they must be young men
who would not go the plain way.
Shadowed, how they twist, how the light
cut off turns them to the light again.
(Earth, how they sword her,
how her black sea floats them.
They plunge the sun into her.)

If the flowers could ask me,
I would want to dream their dreams with them one night.
How simple it must be to flower!
What is there to it but to let light in,
light, first, simple love, palpable, everywhere

descending, from before the broken garden.
I would dream of someone bending
as I bend over us, watching, tasting,
his breath in my throat, wondering how the bee feels,
how I fill the field.
My love comes and I can tell him nothing.
Arms of the night press me.
Rain licks me open.
When I awake the sky is clear above me.
Lord, who so simple made the flowers,
so laborious made me,
You were wrong to suppose that out of
the tasks and missteps I should want,
at the end, anything but death.
I have earned something of the flowers,
some mortal gratitude.
Oh. how they lie back sweetly to their sleep.

In April I stand in the wood with them.
Not with skin, but with the mist
at the ends of fingers, I touch petal, sepal,
stamen, calyx, the dark gun breeding at the heart.
I praise.
I will let them have me when I lie down.
I take them as far as I'm going,
farther, find their way.
I have earned something that if put to words
is as it is to stand with them at morning.
Light calls, they leap up.
Teach me, I will say,
little fires at my ankles like the stars.

THE
JUNIPER
PRIZE

This volume is the seventh recipient
of the Juniper Prize,
presented annually by the
University of Massachusetts Press
for a volume of original poetry.
The prize is named in honor of Robert Francis,
who has lived for many years at
Fort Juniper, Amherst, Massachusetts.